EDINBURGH

First published in Great Britain in 1993 by
Colin Baxter Photography Ltd
Grantown-on-Spey
Morayshire, PH26 3NA
Scotland

British Library Cataloguing in Publication Data
Baxter, Colin
Edinburgh
I. Title
914.13404
Cased ISBN 0-948661-32-1
Paperback ISBN 0-948661-33-X

Front Cover Photograph THE CITY FROM SALISBURY CRAGS
Back Cover Photograph THE SCOTT MONUMENT

EDINBURGH

Photographs by
Colin Baxter

Colin Baxter Photography, Grantown-on-Spey, Scotland

INTRODUCTION

In Edinburgh the dramatic is never far to seek, with long vistas of hill, sea, wood and townscape appearing, sometimes quite unexpectedly, as you turn a corner or breast a hill. Volcanic action of a distant era and glacial carving of a less remote ice age provided a natural fortification for the early city and created the spectacular landscape of modern Edinburgh. Few cities have miniature mountains right at their very centre, such as are the Castle Rock, Arthur's Seat and the Calton Hill, all connected with a series of old volcanoes of the Carboniferous Era, some 360 million years ago. The last ice age was by comparison quite recent at 11,000 years ago; as its great glaciers moved across these hills they left behind a sharply steep west face and an eastward sloping mound of rubble and debris, forming what is known to geologists as crag-and-tail. Partly because of these hills, Edinburgh is very fortunate in its open spaces, not least in Princes Street Gardens below the Castle Rock, overlooked by its single-sided shopping street. Formerly the Nor Loch, this area was drained in the eighteenth century to facilitate access to new developments on the undulating ground northwards towards the Firth of Forth.

The medieval city, now known as the Old Town, had by then outgrown its narrow site on the steep slopes of the ridge from Castle to Palace. It housed all classes of society in high-rise buildings known as tenements or lands, and overcrowding eventually created conditions which caused offence even to the less fastidious. The cry of 'gardyloo' (from French 'garde à l'eau', beware of the water) had to be regarded as a dire warning to passers-by below, as sewage was poured into the street each night. Plans were set afoot in the 1760s for great expansion to the north, in the development still known as the New Town, and building began about a decade later. Though extension was delayed by the Napoleonic Wars and the subsequent recession, by the 1830s one of the finest and most extensive areas of Georgian architecture to be found anywhere had emerged. Much of it still remains, a surprising proportion of it in residential use, giving comfortable, elegant living space close to the city centre, such as can be found in few cities these days.

Meanwhile large parts of the Old Town were falling into decay and massive rebuilding took place, sweeping away medieval structures in a manner which would horrify today's conservationists. Further large-scale changes took place in the mid-twentieth century, but these include excellent restoration of some of the remaining older buildings. It is often said that the majority of the buildings of the New Town are now older than most of the buildings of the Old Town. Some of the nineteenth-century rebuilding however was not unsuccessful. Many of the tenements were built in a style known as Scottish Baronial, derived from the historic Scottish tower house, and also widely used for country mansions; its main features are crow-stepped gables and pepperpot turrets, which, while they may have seemed pretentious at the time, have a pleasing appearance, especially in silhouette.

Both the Old Town and the New are dominated by the Castle, as indeed is the whole history of the city. It had always been assumed that such an ideal site would have had forts built on it from very early times but until very recently there was no direct evidence of building before the sixth century AD. In the late 1980s, however, large-scale engineering works (to provide better visitor facilities) created a marvellous opportunity for excavation; exciting archaeological discoveries were made, including evidence of habitations dating back to the late Bronze Age in the ninth century BC, and later Iron Age dwellings containing Roman as well as native artefacts. These excavations also revealed information about later times, for example the extent of rebuilding after sieges in the sixteenth and seventeenth centuries.

Although Edinburgh did not become officially the capital of Scotland till the seventeenth century, it was one of the principal homes of the Kings of Scots from the eleventh century and became the seat of the Scottish parliament. The medieval court provided a focus for cultural life and when in 1603 King James VI succeeded Queen Elizabeth of England and became the first king of the United Kingdom, the court moved to London, thus depriving the city of this focus. The Calvinism of the Scottish Reformation also had a dampening effect on certain aspects of Scottish life which some consider to be felt to this day. The influence of the church, though much reduced in the late twentieth century, is still in evidence; for one week every May the General Assembly of the Church of Scotland brings ministers and elders from all parts of Scotland to the city.

Edinburgh is also the centre of Scotland's legal system, and the supreme lawcourts, the Court of Session and the High Court of Justiciary, have their seats in Parliament House, just behind St Giles' Cathedral, where the seventeenth-century Parliament Hall is still used by lawyers and their clients. Education also plays an important role in the life of the city and it now has three universities. The University of Edinburgh, founded in 1582, is the youngest of Scotland's four medieval universities and the only one which was not an ecclesiastical foundation; it was originally known as the 'Tounis College', with a charter from the town council. It still has its main campus close to the Old Town. Heriot-Watt University and Napier University have been formed in recent decades from technical colleges.

Although it lost much of its political significance at the Union of the Parliaments with England in 1707, Edinburgh's intellectual

life flourished in the eighteenth century in quite a remarkable way in what later became known as the Scottish Enlightenment. In the middle of the eighteenth century, an Englishman in Edinburgh was heard to say: 'Here I stand at what is called the *Cross of Edinburgh*, and can, in a few minutes, take fifty men of genius by the hand.' These included David Hume, one of the greatest philosophers of modern times, the economist Adam Smith, the author of *The Wealth of Nations*, Adam Fergusson, now regarded as the founder of sociology, the great historian William Robertson, Principal of Edinburgh University and a minister of the Kirk, James Hutton, founder of modern geology, the chemist Joseph Black; the medical school founded by distinguished teachers like William Cullen and Alexander Munro is still world famous.

Literary life flourished, and in the early years of the next century it was dominated by the genius of Sir Walter Scott, whose Waverley novels made their impact far beyond Scotland. Somewhat earlier, in the 1780s, Robert Burns was lionized by the Edinburgh literati during visits to Edinburgh. Not long before, Edinburgh's most gifted poet, Robert Fergusson, had died a pauper's death in an asylum, but his poetry gives one of the most vivid pictures of life in the city in the late eighteenth century. In our own time a similar poetic tribute to the city was paid by Robert Garioch. Both of them, like Burns, were at their most expressive in Scots, a language akin to English and still heard in the streets of the city.

The language, with other aspects of the city, was viewed nostalgically a century later by Robert Louis Stevenson from his distant exile in Samoa. His heart remained in his native city, even if his delicate health could not withstand the rigours of the Edinburgh climate, which he described vividly: 'The weather is raw and boisterous in winter, shifty and ungenial in summer and a downright meteorological purgatory in the spring.' Many today will sympathize as the cold sea fog, known as the haar, seeps in from the east and envelops the walls, creating a chilly but picturesque greyness. But the grey colour of the buildings is in many cases only skin-deep, caused by years, in some cases centuries of the smoke and soot which gave Edinburgh one of its nicknames, Auld Reekie (Old Smoky), much deserved in the pre-Clean Air Act days. The building stone actually has a variety of colours, yellow (or honey-coloured), orange, brown, red, according to which quarry they originated from. These have become clearer recently, with the rash of stone-cleaning in the 1960s and 70s, a practice now somewhat less favoured because of the damage caused to stonework.

Another nickname is 'The Athens of the North', partly from its fame as an intellectual force in the eighteenth century and partly from its spectacular appearance with ancient buildings on a central hill. The origin of the name Edinburgh itself has been much disputed. In the language of the ancient Britons who once peopled this area, it was 'Din Eidyn', the fort of Eidyn, probably their name for the area. This is echoed in the modern Gaelic name, 'Dun Eideann' (anglicized in Dunedin in New Zealand), and Edinburgh is a Germanic form. The theory that it was 'Edwin's burg', the fort of Edwin, a seventh-century king of Northumbria, is not tenable, although this form is found in medieval records.

In the throng of the city it is often easy to forget how close Edinburgh is to the sea, with the Firth of Forth only a mile or two from the city centre. The two great bridges, the Forth Railway Bridge and the Forth Road Bridge, span the river near Edinburgh's western boundary, and to the north is the port of Leith, until quite recently a separate town and still independent of Edinburgh in many of its attitudes. It has been a busy port since the days of Scotland's trade with Europe in medieval times and has imported wine from Bordeaux since the thirteenth century. Claret was at one time more of a national drink than whisky, though the latter also makes its presence felt in Leith, for instance in the home of the Scotch Malt Whisky Society which supplies the finest-quality malts to its members.

Trade, along with the professions, has always had an important role in the city's economy, though manufacturing too has played its part, especially in the brewing and printing industries, so that Edinburgh became known for the 'three Bs': beer, books and banking. Of the three, beer has been much reduced, as have printing and publishing, and only banking has survived at any significant level. Indeed there is a concentration of financial institutions in the city, making Edinburgh one of Europe's important financial centres.

Tourism has grown in importance and Edinburgh has become one of the busiest tourist centres in Britain. Visitors flock to the city the year round, but their numbers reach a peak in August for the Edinburgh International Festival, since 1947 one of the world's most varied and prestigious cultural events, embracing the visual arts and literature, as well as music and drama. Around the core of the official Festival has grown up a series of others, notably the Edinburgh Festival Fringe, which from small beginnings in the early years has grown so that in the 1990s it had over 11,000 performances in about 150 venues.

Colin Baxter's photographs have made many people take a new look at scenery, not only in the countryside but in urban landscapes as well. This book portrays a great city in all its variety and in many of its moods, giving prominence to its contrasts and above all its beauty. Old and new, buildings and natural features, seasonal changes, all conspire to make the heart of Edinburgh an endlessly fascinating urban stage. Even in the age of the peripheral shopping mall and packaged tourism, it sustains a vigorous civic life rooted in the community sense of its people. Long may it continue to do so.

Iseabail Macleod

THE OLD TOWN

*The medieval tower of St Giles' literally crowns the scene of Old Town
tenements opposite. The many-chimneyed roof above reminds us of heating methods
of another age.*

EDINBURGH SKYLINE

*Here centre stage is held by the Scott Monument, surely the most
impressive memorial to a writer anywhere. But the fame of Sir Walter Scott went well
beyond his homeland. This Gothic pile of fantastic intricacy was designed by George
Kemp, a local carpenter, who died before it was completed.*

MELVILLE STREET

RAMSAY GARDEN

This group of houses takes its name from the eighteenth-century poet
Allan Ramsay (father of the portrait-painter) and it adjoins the octagonal house he had
built for himself. The later red and white terraces were designed in the 1890s for
Patrick Geddes, the father of modern town planning, and today provide
elegant living space at the very core of historic Edinburgh.

ARTHUR'S SEAT AND SALISBURY CRAGS

Few cities have a small mountain right at their very centre. Although this core
of an old volcano is only 251 metres high, its rugged steep sides are rough to climb but
worth the effort for the panoramic view from the top.

THE CITY AT NIGHT FROM THE WEST

*The Castle shines out against the backdrop of Arthur's Seat, across the
rooftops of the West End. Also conspicuous are the domes of the Bank of Scotland and
of St George's Church (now West Register House), with the Dean Education
Centre in the foreground.*

CHARLOTTE SQUARE NORTH SIDE

CHARLOTTE SQUARE SOUTH SIDE

*Domestic Georgian architecture in the city reached a fine flowering in this handsome
square, designed by Robert Adam in 1791. Numbers 5, 6 and 7 on the north side are now
owned by the National Trust for Scotland, who have opened the lower floors of No. 7 as the Georgian
House, furnished in the style of its period. The upper floors are the official residence of the
Moderator of the General Assembly of the Church of Scotland and No. 6
is that of the Secretary of State for Scotland.*

OLD TOWN ROOFTOPS AND SPIRES

*Seen from the Outlook Tower the height of Old Town buildings is
emphasized, continuing the medieval tradition of multi-storey dwellings built onto
the steep slope of the hill.*

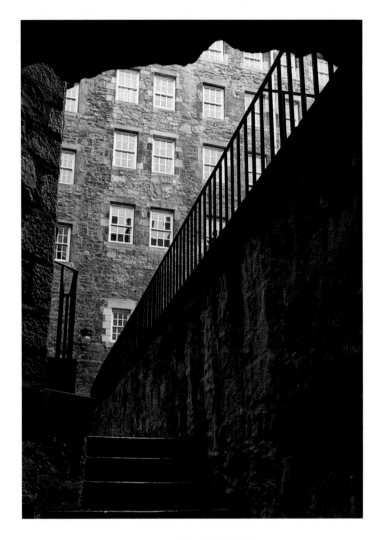

MILNE'S COURT

An early example of slum clearance and courtyard planning in late seventeenth-century Edinburgh. Old buildings were replaced by elegant upper-class tenements. Today it houses University halls of residence.

WAVERLEY

PEN
THE WORLD'S FAVOURITE

WAVERLEY
THE
"BOON & BLESSING" PEN

THE
WAVERLEY PEN
MACNIVEN & CAMERON LTD
EDINBURGH

MACNIVEN & CAMERON LTD. EDINBURGH

WAVERLEY

THE WORLD-FAVOURITE
PEN

6d & 1s PER BOX   AT ALL STATIONERS
They come as a boon and a blessing to men
The Pickwick, the Owl, and the Waverley Pen"
MACNIVEN & CAMERON, LTD.   EDINBURGH

THE
BOONS & BLESSING

THE
PICKWICK   OWL   WAVERLEY

"They come as a Boon and a Blessing to
The Pickwick, the Owl, and the Waverley

WEST NICOLSON STREET   *ELM ROW*

BLAIR STREET
The traditional signs have alas now disappeared.

27

THE CITY FROM THE EAST

*The Castle, as always, dominates the skyline; it is a mixed collection of
buildings from many ages, on a superb, naturally-fortified site. Along with traces of
Iron Age forts, it has medieval fortifications, a Renaissance palace, eighteenth-century
military buildings, and many later additions, including a restaurant
opened in 1992.*

BALMORAL HOTEL CLOCK TOWER

The clock above this Edwardian edifice for generations safeguarded (or alarmed)
hurrying travellers to Waverley Station by always being set a little fast.

FESTIVE FLAGS

Castlehill is bedecked with the city's castle flag for the Edinburgh Festival.
Opposite: The Castle broods over Princes Street Gardens, formed after the drainage of the Nor
Loch, which once filled the hollow below the Castle and hindered contact between the Old Town
and the New Town to the north. It is hard to believe that Edinburgh's main railway line,
carefully hidden, runs through this peaceful scene.

THE CASTLE AND PRINCES STREET GARDENS

31

GEORGE HERIOT'S SCHOOL

*George Heriot's School is seen across the Victorian tenements of the
Grassmarket. It was founded in the 1620s from money left to the city by George
Heriot (the Jingling Geordie of Sir Walter Scott's* The Fortunes of Nigel)*, who was
goldsmith and moneylender to James VI and his Queen, Anne of Denmark.*

LAWNMARKET

This shopfront doorway has a small image of Bonnie Prince Charlie,
Prince Charles Edward Stuart, who led the Jacobite Rising of 1745 and held
court at Holyrood Palace, though his army failed to capture the Castle.

THE BALMORAL HOTEL

The hotel forms a focal point at the east end of Princes Street.
Originally the North British Hotel, it towers above Waverley Station, for whose former
owners, the North British Railway Company, it was built in 1902.

THE MEADOWS AND SPIRES FROM BRUNTSFIELD LINKS

36

HERIOT ROW

CITY SKYLINE AT DUSK

Edinburgh through the ages appears in silhouette here: its ancient
fortress on the Rock, its medieval High Kirk and many later towers and tenements.
Opposite: Ramsay Garden as seen from the National Gallery of Scotland.

JOHN KNOX HOUSE

*Although its connections with the religious reformer John Knox are
unproven, this building is an excellent reminder of what the High Street was like
in his day in the sixteenth century. The initials IM and MA on the coat of arms stand
for James Mossman, goldsmith to Mary, Queen of Scots, and his wife
Mariota Arres, who inherited the building in 1556.*

NORTH BRIDGE AT NIGHT

The North Bridge was the first link between the Old Town and the New
in the eighteenth century and is still one of the main points of contact. It was rebuilt at
the turn of the century and has recently been painted once again in the original Victorian colours.
Opposite: The dusk is brightened by the floodlit Castle and by the Christmas tree on the Mound,
the other main access point from the Old Town, built of the earth and rubble from the
building sites of the New Town.

CALTON HILL AND THE FIRTH OF FORTH
The domes and monuments of the Calton Hill, dominated by the Nelson Monument,
look across the Forth to the hills of Fife. Opposite: The
Calton Hill from Bank Street.

THE MEADOWS

*The Meadows, originally the common grazing land of Edinburgh, form a
delightful tree-lined open space just to the south of the city centre, bound on the north
by the Royal Infirmary and the University of Edinburgh and to the south by
the tenements of Marchmont.*

NEWINGTON FROM SALISBURY CRAGS

OLD TOWN ROOFTOPS

JOHN KNOX HOUSE

CANONGATE KIRK

HOLYROOD

The figure on the corner of the John Knox house represents Moses
pointing to the sun. The royal arms on the Canongate Kirk are a reminder that
it was built, in 1688, by order of King James VII. The Holyrood heraldic panel
with the royal arms of King James V was originally over the gatehouse
which stood at the bottom of the Canongate.

PALACE OF HOLYROODHOUSE

Holyrood Abbey was one of the religious houses which was a frequent
lodging of the medieval Kings of Scots before James IV first built a palace here in 1501.
In fact most of the present building was built after the monarchs had departed to London. Today it
receives regular royal visits, especially every June when garden parties are held in the grounds.
From the air Sir William Bruce's elegant seventeenth-century courtyard and tower can be
clearly seen, with the early sixteenth-century tower on the left.

PRINCES STREET

QUEEN STREET

Recent conservation has highlighted the Georgian elegance of New Town doors;
the fanlights have much variety within the pattern of an overall symmetry.

THE CITY FROM CALTON HILL

FIREWORKS FROM CALTON HILL

*Since the mid 1980s a spectacular fireworks display above the Castle has
been enjoyed during the Edinburgh Festival in August by visitors and residents; it is
sponsored by the Glenlivet whisky company and is accompanied by Handel's Music for the Royal
Fireworks played in the Ross Open Air Theatre below. The city assumes a carnival atmosphere
as crowds gather not only in Princes Street but at more distant vantage points
such as the Calton Hill and Inverleith Park.*

COWGATE

The Cowgate is seen here against the outline of the George IV Bridge above.
This street now has little reminder of its past as an elegant suburb of the medieval city.

TOWARDS THE CALEDONIAN HOTEL FROM THE MOUND

INDIA STREET

These elegant entrances are fine examples of Georgian Edinburgh.
The New Town was planned in the eighteenth century to allow vital expansion from
the overcrowded city on the hill. It produced an extensive area of Georgian
architecture unsurpassed anywhere.

CHARLOTTE SQUARE

VICTORIA
STREET

WEST
BOW

PINE & OLD LACE

46

44 DEAD HEAD COMICS

VICTORIA STREET

*Name and style proclaim its origins in the nineteenth century when it was
built to provide better access to the Old Town from the south. Today it has little
restaurants and small specialist shops.*

THE ROYAL COMMONWEALTH POOL AND NEWINGTON

THE MEADOWS AND MARCHMONT
The busy shopping area around Clerk Street is separated by the Meadows
from the forest of Victorian tenements which is Marchmont, the happy hunting
ground of flat-hunters.

THE BANK OF SCOTLAND

On its commanding site, the bank's headquarters combine the classical
features of the original early nineteenth-century building with the more florid style
of the later Victorian parts.

LOOKING FROM THE CASTLE TOWARDS THE FIRTH OF FORTH

THE FORTH ROAD BRIDGE

The Forth Road Bridge at sunset, looking west from North Queensferry.
Opposite: Edinburgh's Christmas face is more elegant than that of many cities.
Christmas tree lights brighten the open space at the top of the Mound and shine across to
Princes Street, where further lights entice shoppers into the stores opposite.

THE NATIONAL GALLERY OF SCOTLAND AND SPIRES

NATIONAL GALLERY COLUMNS

*W H Playfair's neo-classical building with its Ionic columns forms
a magnificent centrepiece to Princes Street Gardens. It is a fitting home for its
exceptionally fine collection of paintings, with examples of many ages of British and
European art up to the late nineteenth century, along with comprehensive
Scottish collections.*

EDINBURGH UNIVERSITY AND THE PENTLAND HILLS

The towers of the University of Edinburgh look out towards
unusually snowy Pentland Hills. Opposite: The Old Town slopes
down from the Castle, giving a clear impression of the
cramped space on the steep hill.

FRINGE OFFICE

*The Edinburgh Festival Fringe is one of the most exciting events in
the arts calendar. It has grown from a small adjunct to the official Festival
in the early days to a gigantic 11,000 performances in the 1990s.*

FRINGE VENUE

The main principle of the Fringe is that anyone can take part,
anyone that is who has the spirit, energy and wherewithal to mount a show,
large or small, in competition with so many others. This means that all kinds of
premises are called in for duty as venues, from theatres to church halls
to any small corner that can be comandeered.

73

WARDROP'S COURT   *JAMES COURT*

The entrance to Wardrop's Court looks through to Blackie House,
a late seventeenth-century tenement, restored in 1894 and renamed for Professor
J S Blackie. James Court is another fine restoration of a courtyard which itself replaced
slums in the eighteenth century. The philosopher David Hume lived here for a time,
and later James Boswell, who entertained Samuel Johnson here en route for their
Hebridean tour in 1773.

OLD TOWN SKYLINE AGAINST SALISBURY CRAGS

DEAN VILLAGE FROM THE DEAN BRIDGE

DEAN VILLAGE

Nestling along the Water of Leith below the majestic span of the
Dean Bridge, the village grew up around the flour mills which had used the river's
water power for centuries. Today it is a popular residential area, with
houses which are mostly more picturesque than spacious.

THE OLD TOWN FROM THE CASTLE ESPLANADE
Old Town roofs face the Edwardian heights of the Balmoral Hotel.
The background appearance of the Firth of Forth reminds one of Edinburgh's
proximity to the sea. Opposite: The Nelson Monument towers
above Regent Terrace.

THE CASTLE AND PRINCES STREET GARDENS

ST GILES' AND OLD TOWN ROOFS

THE FORTH ROAD AND RAILWAY BRIDGES
The immense cantilevered structure of the railway bridge was a marvel of
engineering when it was built a century ago and still today it is an impressive
giant. Opened in 1964, the road bridge with its very different
structure is also a major feat of modern engineering.

PRINCES STREET AT DUSK

From the Calton Hill, Princes Street sweeps towards the towers of the
West End, with the triple spires of St Mary's Cathedral closing the view.
Opposite: Snow gives a 'grim-fortress' appearance to the Castle walls,
steeply stark above the deserted Gardens.

WHITEHORSE CLOSE

HOLYROOD ROAD

Victorian tenements contrast with the restored charm of Whitehorse Close,
off the Canongate. Formerly White Horse Inn, it was the starting point for the
stagecoach to London, a journey originally lasting eight days.

THE MILITARY TATTOO

For many, the Military Tattoo on the Castle Esplanade is the highlight of the Edinburgh International Festival in August and September. Military groups from all over the world perform music, drill, gymnastics and dancing. The playing of a lone piper on the Castle rampart closes the performance.

THE MOUND

*The garden at the head of the Mound, above Princes Street Gardens,
usually displays an appropriate flower motif, here the Jean Cocteau logo of the
Edinburgh International Festival. Opposite: Flags to the rear of the Royal Scottish
Academy proclaim Festival art, just one of its many facets, with music
and drama sharing the lead.*

THE ROYAL SCOTTISH ACADEMY

ST GILES'

The fifteenth-century crown tower is all that remains of the
medieval external masonry of St Giles'; most of the rest of the exterior dates
from early nineteenth-century restoration. Opposite: Snow has briefly etched out the
nineteenth-century character of later Old Town tenements, distinctively Scottish
with their crow-stepped gables. Salisbury Crags rise steeply behind.

THE SCOTT MONUMENT AND PRINCES STREET

THE OLD TOWN AND CASTLE AT NIGHT

INDEX OF PLACES

Arthur's Seat	18, 19, 21	Meadows	19, 36, 46, 63
Balmoral Hotel	7, 14, 29, 34, 35, 52, 78, 84	Melville Street	15
Bank of Scotland	21, 64	Military Tattoo	88, 89
Blackie House	74	Milne's Court	25
Blair Street	26	Mound	43, 66, 90
Bruntsfield Links	36	National Gallery of Scotland	68, 69
Caledonian Hotel	57, 68	Nelson Monument	44, 45, 79
Calton Hill	44, 45, 54, 79	Newington	47, 62
Canongate Kirk	49	New Town	15, 22, 23, 37, 53, 58, 59, 65
Castle	4, 14, 20, 21, 28, 31, 39, 43, 55, 70, 80, 85, 88, 89, 95	North Bridge	42
Castlehill	30	Old Town	12, 13, 24, 25, 40, 41, 48, 49, 70, 72, 74, 75, 78, 81, 86, 92, 93
Charlotte Square	22, 23, 59	Pentland Hills	42, 71
Cowgate	56	Princes Street	52, 84, 94
Dean Education Centre	21	Princes Street Gardens	31, 80, 85
Dean Village	76, 77	Queen Street	53
Elm Row	27	Ramsay Garden	11, 16, 17, 38, 75
Forth Railway Bridge	82, 83	Regent Terrace	79
Forth Road Bridge	67, 82	Royal Commonwealth Pool	62
Forth, Firth of	45, 65, 67, 78, 82, 83	Royal Scottish Academy	91
George Heriot's School	32	Salisbury Crags	18, 75, 92
George IV Bridge	56	Scott Monument	7, 14, 84, 94
Georgian House	22	St Giles' Cathedral	12, 70, 75, 81, 93
Heriot Row	37	St Mary's Cathedral	84
Holyrood	8, 49, 50, 51	University of Edinburgh	71
Holyrood Road	87	Victoria Street	60, 61
India Street	58	Wardrop's Court	74
James Court	74	West End	21
John Knox House	40, 41, 49	West Nicolson Street	27
Lawnmarket	33	West Register House	21
Marchmont	47, 63	Whitehorse Close	86